Art of Repairing Broken Pottery

by Maggie Hess

The Scream

I was born screaming.
Count me in!
Life let me fly on your back,
into the sun!
I am free!
Here I am!

I was born screaming.
But my lips would not part.
I was made speechless
by the noose,
lassoed around my sweet soft neck,
a symbol of Mom and me collaborating.

But Mom and Daddy
had a competent midwife,
who knew what to do.
So my scream be heard at last:
"waaaaaaaaaaaa!"

Deciding Samsara

The snake eats its head.
The artist births herself.

Which is the universe,
creative or destructive?

Maybe both.
Maybe we decide.

Unmute Yourself

How we are born conditions our whole life.
But we don't have to be trapped by samsara,
the umbilical chord around our neck,
or in the pattern of smothering.

I was born that way, a blue baby,
delivered by a midwife named Doctor Alice
who cut off the line from my mother
that nearly extinguished my life.

I want to say how the cycles of how we are born
can repeat in our life,
but the ways that come to mind make me feel
like a victim blaming oppressors.

Let me just speak generally.
The air has not always been here,
the air is not here,
but I swim for the surface with all my power.

O2 Rhymes

I remember breaths of air,
flowing locks of graying hair,
starlings high upon a wire,
hay bales looking like tires.

I remember breaths of air,
broken feelings of despair,
tiredness, the end of days,
yet hope from something in me stays.

I remember breaths of air,
in the poems that I share,
and in the ones my fingers tare
or truths just send up in prayer.

I remember breaths of air,
maybe I will name them there,
where they rise with dust
or invisible but sure as trust.

Sun Faced Buddha, Moon Faced Buddha

If life was just one day,
I wouldn't sleep at night,
I'd walk barefoot over the beach,
feast with bonfire heathens,
swim on the back of dolphins,
all before noon.
I wouldn't take my medicine,
instead I'd give in to mania,
follow the first stranger to talk to me,
make love with an orgy of mermaids and vagabonds,
whoever caught my attention first.

Moon faced Buddha has one day,
like a single breath is said to live a full life,
my passage would be without stopping or resting,
and maybe that is how we should live every day.

Sun faced Buddha has forever to live,
so takes things more slowly,
enjoys his slumber,
but because death is not imminent,
might never get out of bed.

So as your hair turns white,
remember how short your birthday song may be.

How Morning Energizes

Night seems to drain into the silhouette of trees
Whilst gray sky lightens a backdrop
And some distant bird trills, triumphant.

In the other room I hear you clear your throat,
and I remember throats before,
your mother and how long it took her to swallow.

Some raindrop may station above the head of a robin
one speck reflecting every star and light
might drop through beak into its tilted head.

Barometric Pressure

Mid night can
clear off the
gathering of trees
that circles
around poetry writing.

Maybe it's the moon
waxing and waning
or the candle wax.

A moth will
take a break
from flight
to land on a poet's
tapping finger

before the sun
and butterfly
return again.

Of Rain O're Parched Land

Part of the raining process is writing.
God waters the new peach seedling
only when he is able.

Like God and the peach
My most honest periods
oft come after a long drought.

Writing and Prewriting

If you want me to write something amazing,
I'll need ten days off,
five to stare at the ceiling,
five to watch too much Netflix.
My mind is not just working
when my hands are moving on a keyboard.
There's the actual writing,
and then there's the prewriting.
Prewriting is all the time when I'm not writing
that makes up the main part of the writing.
Thinking you might also call it.
Suffering is a big part of it.
Without feeling deeply the feelings I feel
I won't be able to use the right language
to make my story something other people
might understand in their own experiences.
Misery, that's useful.
But not self inflicted misery.
Unless maybe from eating too many sandwiches
too close to bed time.
Then I get knots in my stomach
it's like some constipation.
It's all writing I say.
Even the worse feeling in the nerves.
Every moment of life
goes into the writing process,
is the writing process.
Those times when my hands are on the keyboard
are just a slim percentage
of the time I need to live in order know what to say.

Naked Originality

If my art lost its integrity,
there would be no more reason.
No heart remaining.
Nothing to uphold.
I could let you take away its dignity.
I could let you walk over top it in charcoal stilettos.
You could throw used diapers on top of it.
While I sat idly by.
But then I'd have lost my purpose too.
My art is one strand of the braid,
inseparable from myself.
Do not corrode me.
I don't need a cover artist.
I don't care how much you pay them.

I might have been missing the purpose of poetry.

Maybe I never picked up on the point of poetry.
I knew reading makes the poet better,
but did I really know?
Did I really read?

To demonstrate my point,
I could write the following poem about this poem:

Crow caws all day,
but when does she look at the water?
A duck,
a bird who knows the pond better,
fowl that's gazed into the reflecting pool
even dunked its head in
I'd listen to a duck lecture on water,
yet it's the crow who never quits talking.

Sea Ars Poetica

See, just sea
what poem comes,
bubbling up,
sloshing in,
waves rising and falling,
bobbing along,
ocean, my emotion
churning over the deck,
what the heck -
a fish -
why not,
fishing for
compliments
alone this morning.
I think I'll bate
my breath
I think I'll wait
throw my net
out into the tide
and watch the shore
for pirates.
Summon up my breath,
the wind,
winding out my reel,
real beautiful sailing along,
under sun and stars.

Ars Poetica 4

Ars Poetica 1 was har har hars poetica

If you just write sounds,
what sounds good might not
have a smart feel too it.

Ars Poetica 2 was Sea Pirate Ars Poetica

Some mornings I check my email
before I write my poems.
It's recommended to write poems first.

"This sucks but the next one wont"
is a valid poetic device.

Ars Poetica 5

I am still trying to wrap my mind around the ars poetica.
So here is an ars poetica ars poetica or
ars poetica squared.
Where an ars poetica explains the "art of poetry"
or meditates upon poetry in poetry,
an ars poetica poetica
is a poem that talks about ars poetica.

To illustrate how the container
can contain another container,
I will bore you with my dreams.

Last night I had a dream
that I was strangling a wolf
so it wouldn't kill me.
I woke from that dream
into another dream
that I was strangling my own dog
accidentally in my sleep.
I woke up and petted my little dog
who was pressed up against
my stomach
to the point it was painful.

A typical ars poetica
contains a poem talking about poetry,
a typical ars poetica squared,
is this poem.

Ars Poetica 6

The young poet
is most valuable
in poetry
because their poetry is fresh,
raw,
jagged.
The mistakes they made
may be seen
as gold
lacing together
a broken pot.
Their split infinitives make older poets smile.
Their mixed metaphors serve important purpose.
Their immature attempt
at least gets the job done
without over thinking
and in that effort
their poetry exceeds masters
at least in that way.

The old poet
writes ars poeticas
tirelessly
trying to write the perfect one.

The too old poet
just works on one poem
day and night
never really writing it down
until their lungs
quit flexing and breathing
gasping for one final slice of
air.

Ars Poetica 7

All ars poetica poetry
should be read in the wry voice
of Billy Collins.

Not all ars poetica poems
are read in the wry voice
of Billy Collins.

Bending aRt
             to put it in the Envelope

Even if the paper is really never folded,
all art gets bent
in the process of passing
it on from the original creator.

I would not recommend intentionally
creasing a masterpiece or
sketch of any kind.

There already is a terrible lack
of museums, books,
or displays for Art.

Too many works
of genius have been balled up
and tossed into too many waste baskets,
and here I am being quite literal.

Mistakes might cause an artist
to throw something away that
could turn the course of someone
else's whole life.

On Gardner's Art Through the Ages, 10th Edition,

Over a thousand pages
all brightly illustrated
with more words than a dictionary
to walk the inquisitive student
through Art History,
but not one mention of
Hilma af Klint,
the first abstract artist.

The reason for writing Hilma af Kilnt
out of art history for the hundred years she most shook
is up to debate,
but is also an obviously simple reason at that
- because she was a woman.
As one friend declared,
behind every man is an amazing woman
of equal or greater talent.

It takes a whole tomb of a book
up to page 1068
before a painting of a woman is ever used,
that of one Georgia O'Keeffe,
as if to say "it is supremely rare for
a woman to make any noteworthy art,
so here is one example
that doesn't happen to be particularly splendid,

and if you are a girl or woman,
you best give up."

Moon

To you I bare my pearls
Every shape you form
I smile up to you,
through seasons,
whether you resemble softball
or half circle,
I grin towards you.

I started showing my teeth
to our celestial orbiting body
a couple weeks ago.
Since that time
I have felt generally more connected
to the larger universe
we share.

Midnight quenching

The poems you write in the middle of the night
seem different,

Like there 'r more there
right there just waiting to flip off the griddle.

Cutting my Nails

I cut my finger nails more than my toes nails.
Toes can have snags
and must be done precisely.
Toe nails can be brittle and soften with bath water.

When I was younger, I didn't cut them over a waste can.
Now I am past the point of what's cute,
and I try to collect them
so they don't sail their little anchors into my favorite rug.

God,
I woke up this morning to see
you left your nail
sailing down its anchor, turning waves.

Zoom in, Zoom out

I am a God.
I am I am.
I am a mirror.
I am the person in the mirror.

To my dog I am a God.
To my cat I am the great giver of Iambs.
To the glass I am another mirror.
I say I am the person, but am I?

Perspective knows everything.
I know but one perspective.
I am what I feel.
Lately, achy, needing motion.

There might be one kid
who calls me a hero.
What does Wilder see in me?
She's big. She is wrapped in skirts of mystery.

Drifting meteors
might say I am next to nothing.
But who else on Earth
is poemizing meteors?

Take that lens of smallness.
Take that lens of mighty.
Take that lens of aching.
Try to know yourself.

Safe Space

You built a safe space,
and right away
you invited people in,
one at a time,
under the tin roof
we listened to the rain
and more and more of us
meant less and less space.

You find us like stray kittens,
collect us like favorite bags,
one by one,
your special ones,
each told true sweet nothings.

You see the good in people.

You elevate our strengths,
and together we hold up more roof,
until it stops raining.

Nothing lasts forever

How can I stretch this good thing I have going on?
Nothing lasts forever,
I know.
So I tried so hard to keep some moments
they withered on the vine.
Other times, it was people
I squashed like June bugs.

Hold tight to your moments,
but let them fly.
Hug your people.
They're just hobbies.

Jittery, nearer to excitement

Chilly evening air.
Just to sit up a couple hours
with a little longer hair.
Some see uneventful,
I see silver linings everywhere.
I've got my second wind now,
writing poetry about the things I care.

Natural Flow of Emotion

I can hit rock bottom every month.
Feeling good can be such a contrast,
but reoccurs again and again.
Coming up out of a deep ocean,
breathing again.

Family Self Portrait

I am a little girl.
I need words that are loud enough and I don't have them.
My siblings play with legos I cannot touch.
No one will play with me.
Daddy is berating Mom.
I am afraid of what it means, of what might happen.
I am afraid of divorce.
I am afraid they don't love each other.
I don't want to think about these things.
I don't have a voice to speak up for my needs.
I am getting lost in the shuffle.

Those memories are just paint.
I am the painting and the painter.
Feelings and colors smeared over me
to dry and chip and bleed.
I might not even remember what lies
beneath my layers.

But I know this painting was folded to make all of my choices.
Origami of a little boat
for me to sit inside.
I am the folder too and the navigator.
I get to decide where this boat takes me,
which way to steer.
How to raise the sail.
If courage musters,
if I find new ways,
if I part from my origin,
that is all up to me.

A Different Psychosis

When I was psychotic
my family needed
to catch me
like I was a wild animal.

Before the psychosis,
in a 15 year stretch
I worked so hard not
to lose control.

I had told them
during those years
that if it ever happened again
they should just call an ambulance.

Their unwillingness
to follow my wishes
came from a place
of love.

They didn't want
whatever handcuffs
or heavy injections
might come with that call.

I may have been psychotic
but more than one
referred to me during that time
as perfectly sweet.

I remember being sweet,
nonviolent, never rough,
but I also remember seeing fear
in my dog's eyes.

I was not responsible.
My family members could not
"manage" me.
My impulses then were causing harm.

When I was psychotic
my family needed
to catch me
like I was a wild animal.

When Mom and Joey
decided I needed the hospital,
Mom came up with a lie
to convince me to go willingly.

You Can't Delete in Life

You can't delete the past.
You obviously can't erase something that happened,
words that were said,
a nightmare or feeling.
But in some rare occasions
I have wanted to.

Maybe the first was high school embarrassment
I could have done without,
wanted to eliminate from my history,
made me feel so horrible,
like I couldn't go on the same,
even small things can have heavy pain.

The worst time I wanted to press delete
was also long ago,
the first morning I woke
knowing my behavior had been
this strange new word "psychotic"
a word maybe I knew before,
but never had myself experienced.

So then, heavily medicated,
I sat there wondering
maybe there was something deeply wrong
about me,
maybe I was not a good person,
maybe there was something broken in my soul.
In that moment, I wished I could subtract that previous week.

Was it just a week?
It seemed so monumental
and yet I could not take it away at all.
It felt like what happened in Indiana
would ruin my life,
and I was trapped with it having happened.
There was no going back or erasing.

Actually, I tried for a very long time
to erase mental illness from how people perceived me
especially publicly.
This created a war within myself
over who I was.
The psychosis, the mania, the erratic decisions, depression,
all were deeply a part of my identity
because they represented my story.
And my trying to erase that part was doing more harm than good.

So I started talking about myself as mentally ill
finally, half way through college.
I opened up for the first time in a class
on Race, Class, Gender, and Sexuality
because I felt that the class should have included
other types of people groups like Disability, and Mental Illness.

But that feeling
was more present in that moment
than any other time
except maybe the next week
and the following month
and even the whole next semester,
because sitting there realizing I was ill
and had been "psychotic"
caused a pain inside of me I had never known.

During that semester,
the anxiety grew and grew
that something might be wrong with me
because of the mental problems.
Not to mention,
I had to take a medicine now
that was so heavy on my thin, small framed body
that was beginning to grow fat
with the weight gain side effect.

My breasts even started randomly lactating,
a side effect that sounds gross
for someone without a child,
and indeed was very hard on my ego,
of someone who had before all that
been successful,
and considered to be pretty and normal.
Those things, pretty, normal, and successful
were deleting from my person,
just as I would have chosen to
press the button of elimination
on the idea of me being mentally ill.

Looking back, though,
after my frame tripling in size,
after taking on the idea and self concept
of mental health advocate,
after having successfully pushed through college,
I consider myself beautiful.
The only one of those that successfully subtracted
was the idea of normal.

Yet, that young version of me,
the one who has just learned she has mental illness
desires so strongly to erase that history
she doesn't know the story of what happened
will form and shape her life
for the better,
because it will open her to a new compassion,
a new way of thinking,
a wiser, stronger picture of who she is.

I want to hold her hand
in a way that surprises her with comfort,
in a way that no one has ever touched her,
in a way that doesn't even require words.
But if words were there for it
they would say
"you can't delete in life
so stop wanting to take away what happened.

It does not have to delete you
that thing of your recent past
you would like to vanish.
It will plant in you a seed of growing,
that very moment when you were psychotic,
that very moment when your Western family members
cried out worrying their daughter was gone,
that you would no longer be the person
you really were,
the girl they had loved.

I want you to find the courage
to raise your voice and say,
you're right.
I'm not that girl anymore.
I am a shaman now."

Waves of Thankfulness

Occasionally I remember a stranger
who helped me so much it changed my life.
Someone put me in connection with my mentor,
and before I could thank her she slipped away.
Someone helped me get home from Costa Rica
the first time, when I was becoming psychotic,
a couple made sure I got to the right terminal,
without them I might still be in the airport.
There was a man who comforted me
after my assault
who sat beside me on the train from Maine
reassuring me in the good of people.

A flood of gratitude comes to me.
I want to thank all the people who helped me.
I am just so grateful.

www.ingramcontent.com/pod-product-compliance
Lightning Source LLC
Chambersburg PA
CBHW071241140726
47996CB00007B/2699